The Architect of Elsewhere

poems by

Donna Wolf-Palacio

Finishing Line Press
Georgetown, Kentucky

The Architect of Elsewhere

For my family and friends

Copyright © 2022 by Donna Wolf-Palacio
ISBN 978-1-64662-976-3 First Edition
All rights reserved under International and Pan-American Copyright Conventions. No part of this book may be reproduced in any manner whatsoever without written permission from the publisher, except in the case of brief quotations embodied in critical articles and reviews.

Publisher: Leah Huete de Maines

Editor: Christen Kincaid

Cover Art: Reynaldo T. Palacio, photographer

Author Photo: Reynaldo T. Palacio

Cover Design: Elizabeth Maines McCleavy

Order online: www.finishinglinepress.com
also available on amazon.com

Author inquiries and mail orders:
Finishing Line Press
PO Box 1626
Georgetown, Kentucky 40324
USA

Table of Contents

Blue Flame 1
Wen 2
Small Window 3
A Place at the Center of the Earth 4
The Architect of Elsewhere 5
A Stone Can be Broken 6
Square Root 8
What They Taught Us 9
The Leavened Heart 10
Scholars 11
My Third Song 12
The Great Elephant 13
Ill-Omened Tools 14
Boat 15
White Fox 16
Jade Snake 17
Drifting 18
Crane 19
Idols 20
Swallows 21
Refugees 22
All This 23
Evening – Second Day of Spring 24
Stars and Books 25
God of Deafness 26
No Poem 27
Mandelbrot and His Fractals 28
Name 29
Small 30
Again 31

Blue Flame

The shadow of what might have been lingers over all of us,
binding us in a flame. The hottest part,
my daughter told me, is the blue part.
It makes sense, since extremes sink back to darkness.
I suppose that is why we imagine ourselves
taking off in dreamy light, flying and landing,
like giddy butterflies clapping the wind.
Is everything unfathomable, infinite, inconceivable?
Or do we simply float in a curve, blind, bending towards flame?

Wen

> "The wen person is someone who can read, not just human language, but the languages of nature."

These are the roads I know, reaching out into the light.
We rush to make ourselves heard among the trees.
Out of light we will make great prospects, we will weave ourselves
an endless net of words in many languages.
The most beautiful, though, is picture after picture.
No waste.

Small Window

I see it again, light on a wire.
Crossings that do not fear the light but free it.
When they break free, they bury the past.

So the huge blind stars know something after all,
how to hang in the sky, night after night, traveling and dangerous,
like lost images you could put your hand through.

Some stars lived in water and always will.
Some dragged themselves out to land, gasping.
It's easier to imitate the dawn than to rush away from it.
But you have to keep odd hours, stay up all night,
one eye on the moon.

A Place at the Center of the Earth

Why is this place different from any other?
Birds may rise in it; silence finds a place here
as if that freedom were its home.
The center of the earth tries to be home to all things.
But it just can't stop changing.

So the solid bright stars look like they could fit into a cup.
One day, like seagulls, they may drop into the waves.
Maybe it would be better to live near the sea.
But when you love a thing, it exerts pull,
and you can rush past riches, seeing nothing but what pulls you.
The earth is full of these mistakes.
But nothing so human can empty the seas.

The Architect of Elsewhere

These leaves, dry and brown,
draw their signature on the wet soil,
the handiwork of winter overcoming fall.
They form a mask,
to help us understand the grip of death
is holding on to the root
one final time while the sun waits and burns.

If the point is to remember, then we're doomed.
But if we live history, then maybe we have a chance.
The tree over this deck fills with bird songs.
Row after row of pachysandra bliss out right up to
the edge of the possible.

Leaves are blind, and branches eat light in darkness.
Roots dig deep and rest. In the middle of the night, a small package,
wrapped like a mirror, arrives. The shards of remembered
daylight blink away the bright full moon.

A Stone Can Be Broken

A stone can be broken, but it cannot become what it is not.
My body wants to soak up sleep,
rewind itself to where it began.

You play a tune under your breath.
You realize someone is playing it for you.
You wander, darkness around you. You take up residence,
a small inextinguishable light.

The crow is back with something new to say.
He calls to other birds, bolder but less permanent.
A wolf of time eating the air.

The moon left its thin crescent mark on the morning
while the sun drove the day.
Everything had purpose, none of it was random.
An old illusion. Grab hold, till you're one with the surface
like all other creatures.

The sky looks like it's ready to cry. Birds play apart from the window.
How light they seem in the darkness.
Even if we were all level, straightened, remorseful,
we would still repeat the past.

It's almost always time to go.
We don't need the crow to tell us.
Yet the crow knows his mind better than anyone.
His lucid dark crow-mind.

Here you are again,
parading around in your empress gown,
big flower on front. Like you owned the place,
little confused diamond.

A face becomes a castle, Does something need to happen?
Isn't it enough the air is an actual thing, something to let go?

Let's name that spirit. Door open. Door shut.
We always hold ourselves in check. We watch golden skies
disappear in the landscape. I used to fly over trees in dreams,
take off and land.

Square Root

This flower must be the square root of something.
Leaves bent into visions, holy vessels, watery,
declaring what they know. They live to try not to die out,
looking for language.

This map has no name. At the end of the day, it rests.
While the line crosses the sky, it has a right to loudness.
Its voice a swarm of stars, torn apart.
It is the loss of dimension.
It makes us more than we think we can be,
while we pretend to find the color of heaven.

Here are these objects again. The wood littered with leaves,
the white table where your shoes wait to be polished.
This all came from the sea.
So we deserve the best possible life.

Does the moon still rise here?
Does the drilling through mountains obey the law of dirt and light?
Are these the wooden animals? Pig, cow, horse?
And are we happy with this line of reasoning?

I returned to the Schuylkill,
how it rushed towards the city, how it proclaimed itself
and did not have to imitate nature. Brushed by the morning traffic,
a prince entering the kingdom.

When the wind rises, we are sleeping and barely notice.
I awake at 3AM. In darkness. I find the deck, and leaves sway
at my feet. Early workers pass. One leaves his cap down over his eyes.
Another enters where the two lights work their way up the walk.
Three trays are bright in their silver emptiness. Cars spin
over the sleepy road. I imagine myself in the tops of the trees,

What They Taught Us

Stay rooted in objects. They are your best friends,
solid, real, unchanging.
So why was I so fixated on disappearing things?
These words, for instance, flooding the page?
Or twilight or the moon, or even, when I'm in the mood,
darkness and night?
Our feet are planted more firmly than we know.
Listen to the bell, its hard final sound. It reminds us:
every sound is infinite.

The Leavened Heart

> *"The mind and leavened heart travel by information."*

The moon in the doorway tries to keep the door open.
It is not in its nature to show us its darkness.
It has to always look like it is moving.
We are told to stay in our places, hold on to whatever light we can find. But we know that no one can close the door that never really opens.

Scholars

Hiding the scars of their struggles
these scholars, old friends, talk sadly
back in the mountains.
This walled city is no greener,
yet it holds what we leave for the people
and their music. At night, people dance and sway,
leave their beds to come hold each other
in the center of this walled city.

My Third Song

> *"Alas, this is my third song.*
> *If I die here, how will you find my bones?"*

The dragon spirit lives in the river.
I live below, where its fierceness cannot see me.
I am alone with the dragon's shadow.
From below come spirits whose home
is deeper than this world. They see what is still alive,
what wildness can still be conquered.
Their slow unfolding lifts the river.
If you stand on the shore, you can almost see it.

The Great Elephant

Scatter and illuminate.
Teach upper and lower.
Lose what you lose.
Stay in the gravelly place
with what remains.
What we know can never be gone.
Propriety follows: this bird, that tree.
Lie beneath the branch that bears fruit
or weeps, if you think it will help.

Ill-Omened Tools

A great victory
is a funeral ceremony.
The parts betray the whole.
Where we walk, sun shines.
When we sleep, moon sleeps
Deep in this history,
We blend sorrow.

Boat

For so many years we have been apart.
Is there a boat coming to your shore?
Wait. This really is the last boat.
No other is coming tonight.
That's not right. In the future,
another is moving slowly on the water,
rocking from side to side.
It tries to come full circle near no boat.

White Fox

> *"A white fox leaps and a yellow one*
> *stands stock still"*

I spin the last wheel.
Lockstep into the eternity of meaning.
The world has changed. No flying thing can escape.
No fence can keep us in.
What goes away comes back,
if it can still get through.

Jade Snake

It jumps off surfaces, lies at a tilt,
almost laughing, then without warning,
it jumps up and presses its snaky body to a tree.
I am the incarnation of beauty, it seems to say,
and no one can prove I am lying.
Purity and flaw are my friends, I love them dearly,
it declares. And I love to scare people away
and then spring into action. Also, I love my tongue.

Drifting

Nothing pulls me towards or away. The summer heat
rocks me. I've gone sleepless for this peace.
Never mind the traffic or the thickness of birds
climbing out of sight.
The speckled tree;
small birds hopping from branch to branch.

Crane

The one-legged crane loves the shore. He tells his story.
The stirring birds have spoken theirs already.
No one places a hand over their mouths.
No one drives a stake into their hearts.
Does this make sense to you? This place
is covered with a thin veil. To see the crane fly
is a miracle. Unless something fixes itself too far in his beak,
he'll find his home.

Idols

Just remember,
though you may knock them down,
others will appear, at another time, another place.
While flowers come and go by season,
idols are the maps of history we cannot erase.
Wherever we find them,
the soil is sacred to somebody.

So be careful, if Fall is coming,
they may lie down in peace.
But in the spring, they will break through
to a new season's split heart.

Swallows

No swallows here,
though in the spring
trees burst with blossoms,
and the wind
is softer, milder.
Inside, in winter
you imagine the wind
and all its blossoms
and its bursting
red and orange
flames; it's what keeps you here,
what you have fought to know.

Refugees

Smooth pine edges of a table.
We look alike, write alike, dream alike.
The man who pushed the girl on the plank into the water.
He was impatient and wanted to survive,
but it is no excuse. Anyway, the man was shot
by the guard. He drowned under the plank.
After that, they crossed one by one.

All This

Light seeps into every corner of the cave,
A wind speaks, a fine harmony, years in the making.

Dreams are warm like the soft grass and the budding willow
with its brown leathery pouches that layer the earth.
The stories we told were dragons in the night. They covered shade
with quiet surrender.
Where is the other?

Does it rain there, where seeds sink in the soft mud for days,
then suddenly burst into green shoots, defying our laws?
I find the mountain, climb, watch flowers appear
and disappear and love the dark woods. In daylight, I free myself of
dragons.
The voice inside lives its own still life, always ready, like a waterfall.

Set back in that cove, the birds sing.
We watch from the pier as they shuffle in and out of the bay. A cool
wind disperses them.
Today the water feels murky and alive, but the birds follow the heat
and live with clouds and shadows near the sunken moon.

How can I not watch? Chill bare branches will soon be green and
able to float.
Clouds cover the sky. We inherit what is left,
the bones, an ordinary day.
Bright yellow daffodils and red tulips throw their heads to the sun.
Soft light drifts over small windows at the back of the house.
A haze of light. The waiting shadow, blur of wire,
disappears into the crossed and uncrossed branches.
A plane rumbles overhead, traffic is a morning song,
a half-made garden.

Evening – Second Day of Spring

1

Street lamp rocks like an old giraffe.
Wet layer of rain coats the ledge.
Shore birds pass through, call
"come, come, come" and "now, now, now",
duck through tall rooftops, riding a draft of wind to the top.

2

Your body humped like a cloud.
Dreamy air turned to a coarse grey castle
raising and lowering its bridge.
This is the wage of wandering apart from the castle,
into the green field, where lying still takes the unquiet body
out of itself. We rise on a blue ladder.
We are flooded with light.

3

The landscape melts, a kind of sleep
almost empty of dream.
In a small wood cove, I make my hands a pillow, watch for dawn.
New light sweeps in, blazing with its final love of shade.

Stars and Books

When darkness leaves, in half-light, you pray
for redemption, trust yourself to the stars,
distant, almost perfect. When we swirl through the universe,
we don't know if our feet will touch ground
or simply fly off to other worlds. Unlikely diaspora,
dreaming the days away in books.
Could you have imagined so many universes?

God of Deafness

Draining the world of its trials,
the god of deafness understood flowers and birds,
but the rest was a mystery. He liked mysteries,
but this one was particularly sticky, so he let me pass,
saying, "you're one brave cookie".
He liked my spunk, me trying to toss my pennies blind.
But he still liked to play god,
and the world was still the world.

No Poem

This is the poem no one composed over water.
No floods off mountains reduced to streams of tears.
Not some lunatic jumping off a cliff humming the Star Spangled Banner.
Not gods at a feast dripping blood all over the linoleum floor.
Those are ridiculous. Wake up already.
Push the veil of tears back. You can hide, but the words
that fade are still yours.

Mandelbrot and His Fractals

"Clouds are not spheres.
Mountains are not cones.
Coastlines are not circles.
Bark is not smooth,
nor does lightning travel in a straight line."

When God said,
"Be fruitful and multiply",
maybe he meant,
Be clouds without edge.
Be mountains without edge.
Be coastlines without edge.

Name

Nature seems endless when you only know one temple.
Place this tray of spring flowers under the window.
Pull up under the old deck where we used to play.
Young trees shadowed the poles out of darkness
in the evening light. We seemed to know
more than we were told. We chalked on the driveway
the names of the ones we loved and then our own mysterious names.

Small

Small red Buddha under porcelain vase.
Orange flowers touch blue stems.
Moments after flying, birds wash in a plain blue pool.
Their chicks break out of speckled bird shells,
eyes closed. In our small tree,
they listen for the wind.

Again

May this tree drop plums,
little round blinking May
fleecy soft bulbs skin clear
smooth drawn by light
to our upturned faces.
If the seed ripens, let it show
more than it sees, like snow
in a field. Let it live
by light, measuring the full air
branch by branch, seed by sky by wind,
till summer comes.

Donna Wolf-Palacio is author of *What I Don't Know, The Other Side*, and *Step Lightly*, published by Finishing Line Press. She taught an ongoing poetry workshop at the University of the Arts and was editor/consultant of the *UARTS Poetry Review*. She has published her writing in *Poetry, The Pennsylvania Gazette, the Musehouse Journal, Intro, The Interpreter, Poems from the Heart: Poems about Adoption,* and *Voices*. She has received grants from the National Endowment of the Humanities, The Leeway Foundation, and the Pennsylvania Council for the Arts. She is a psychotherapist who lives in Philadelphia with her husband and daughter.